Bears, Bea

The first little bear
went scrub, scrub, scrub.
"I'm cleaning the bathroom,
rub-a-dub-dub!"

3

The second little bear went mop, mop, mop. "I'm cleaning the floor, slop, slop, slop!"

5

The third little bear went swish, swish, swish. "I'm washing the plates, whish, whish, whish!"

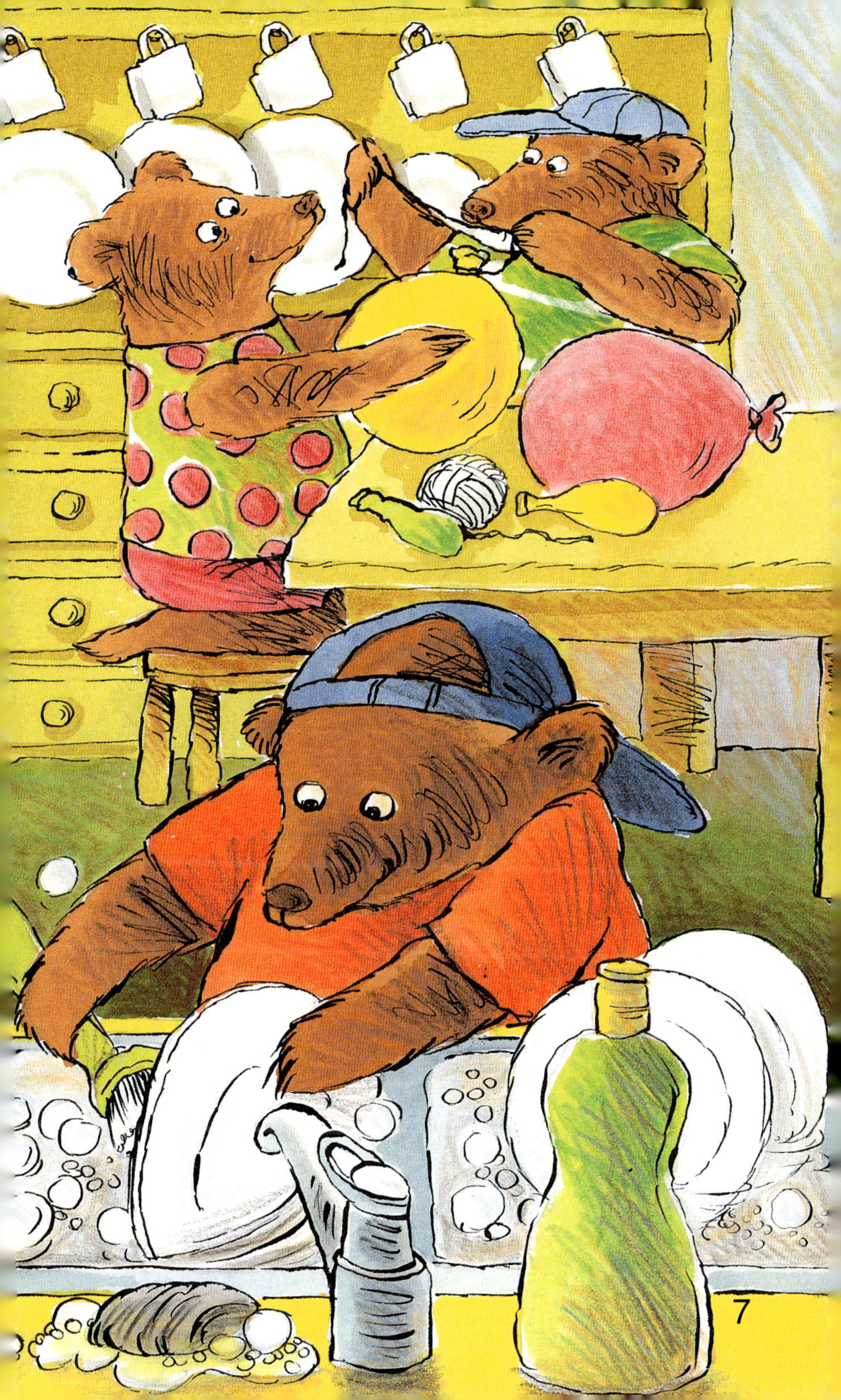

The fourth little bear went stir, stir, stir. "I'm making a cake, whirr, whirr, whirr!"

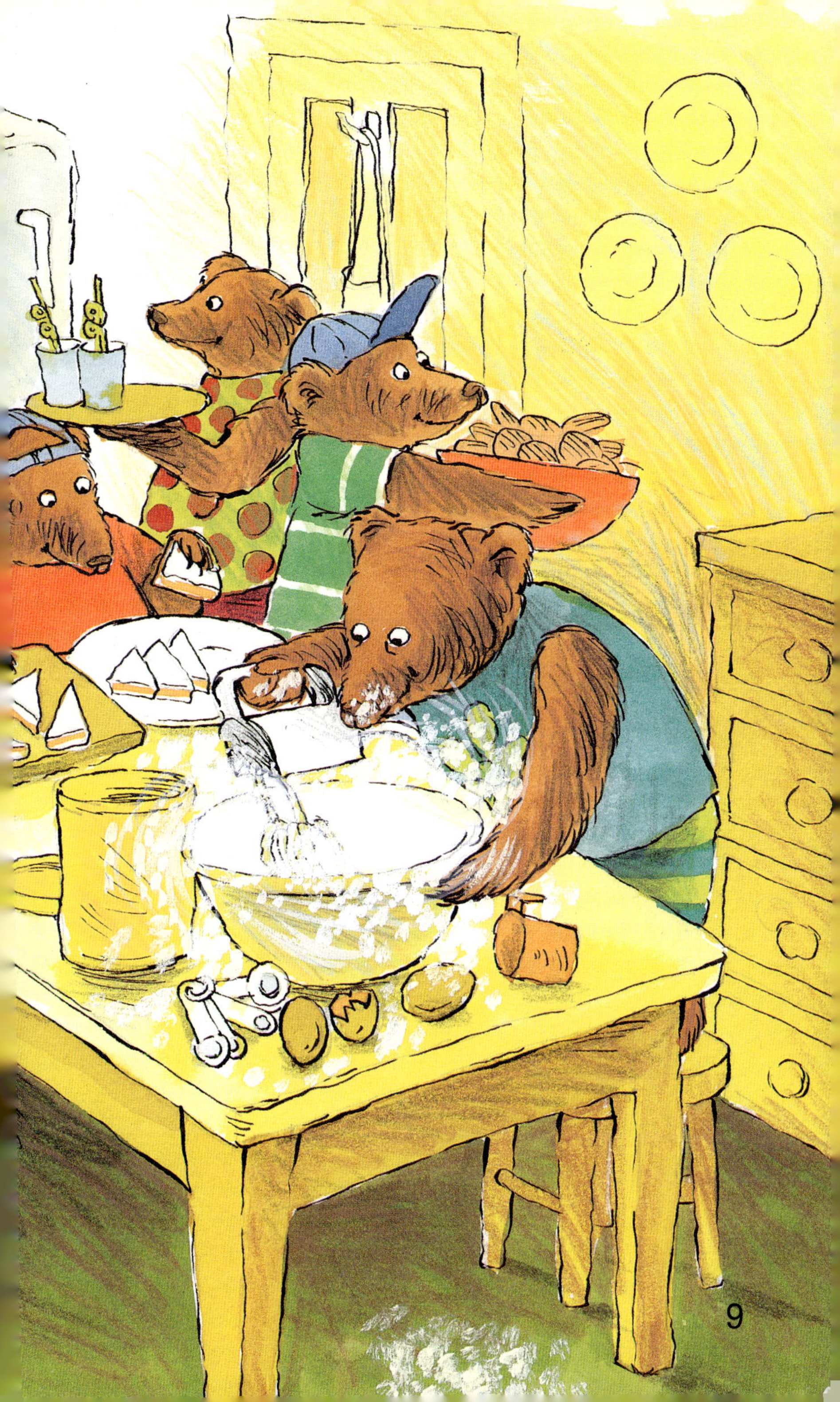

The fifth little bear
went up the stairs.
"Look out the window,
bears, bears, bears!"

11

Five little bears
ran to the door.

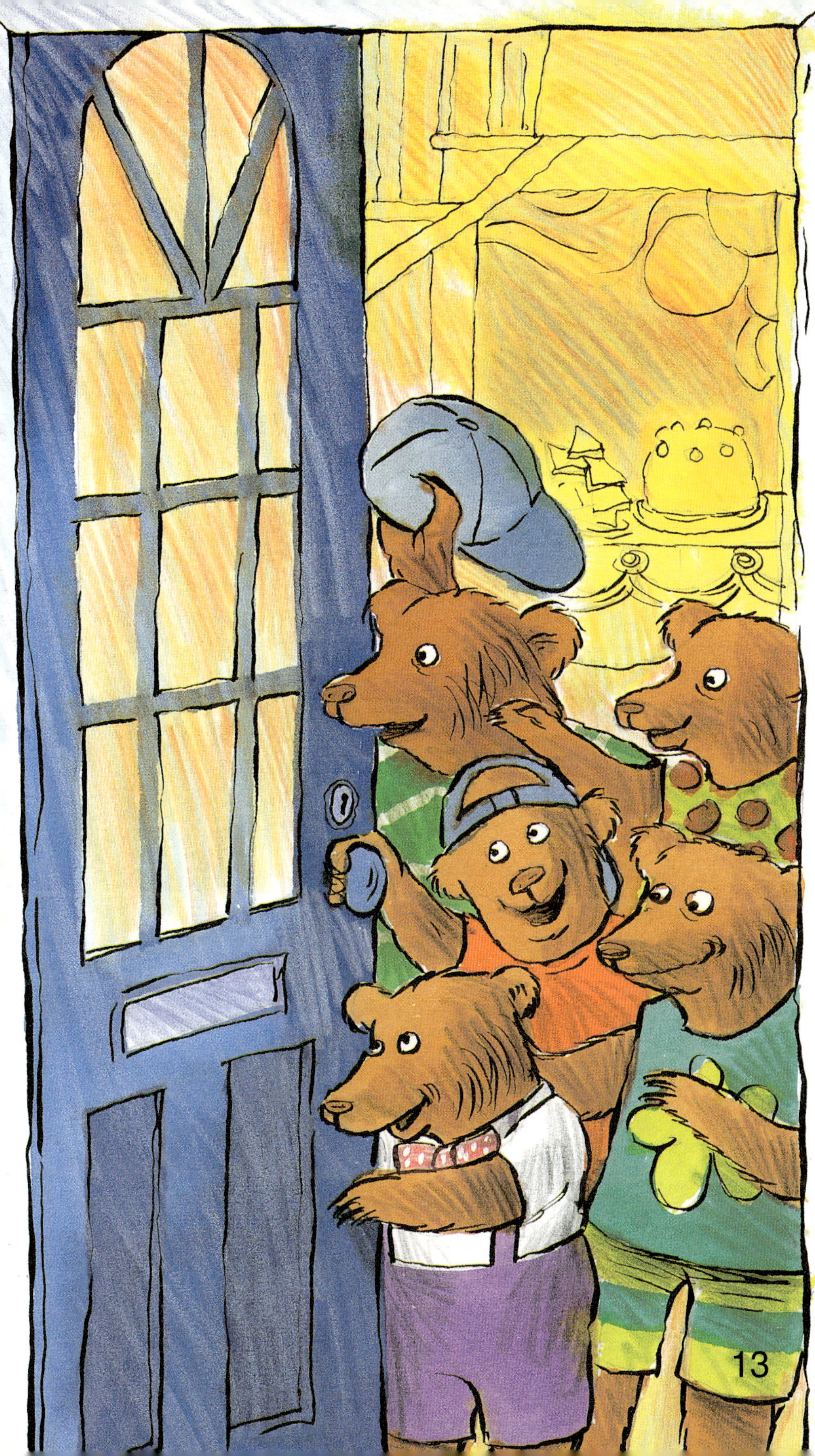

"Come in, bears.
Shake a paw!"

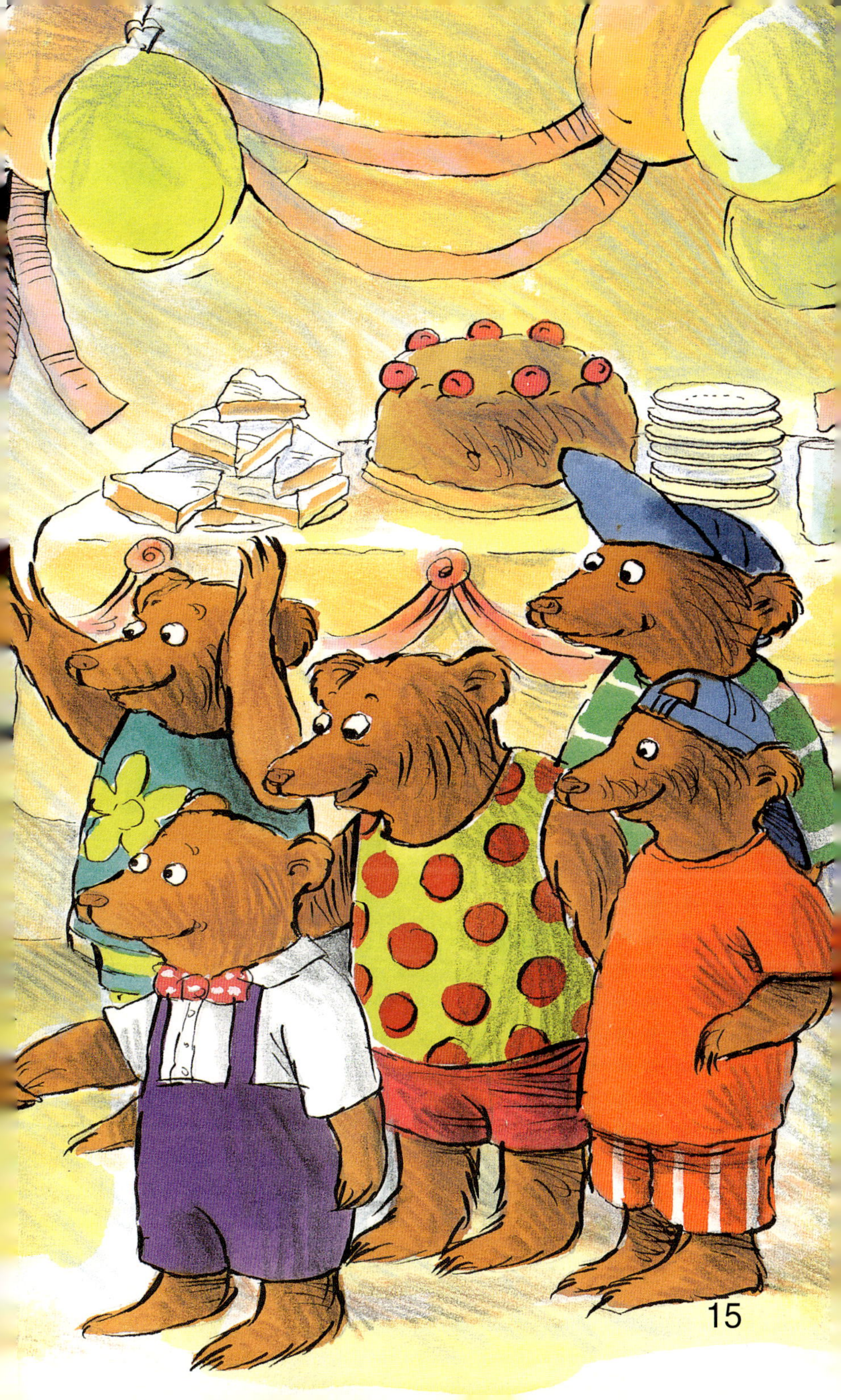

16